Original title:
The Moss Diaries

Copyright © 2025 Creative Arts Management OÜ
All rights reserved.

Author: Dean Whitmore
ISBN HARDBACK: 978-1-80581-913-4
ISBN PAPERBACK: 978-1-80581-440-5
ISBN EBOOK: 978-1-80581-913-4

Stories Beneath the Surface

In a world where green things wiggle,
Moss meets a bug that loves to giggle.
With a little hop and a tiny dance,
They stumble upon a mushroom romance.

Slugs in tuxedos plot a grand feast,
Sipping dew drops, they party, at least!
A caterpillar DJ spins tunes all night,
While crickets provide the disco light.

Under leaves, the ants hold court,
Swapping tales of their last resort.
A beetle in shades claims he's royal,
But all of them tremble at the oil!

When morning comes, the laughter fades,
The mossy ground bears no charades.
With each step, the stories remain,
Whispers of joy in the sun and rain.

Relics of the Underbrush

A snail with dreams of silver and gold,
Wanders beneath a leaf quite old.
He claims he once fought a mighty frog,
But really just napped in the morning fog.

Under twigs where shadows blend,
A squirrel's stash will never end.
With acorns and nuts, he plays a game,
Forgetting the spot, now isn't that lame?

A toad recites poetry with flair,
Each line punctuated by a sweet air.
But slips on a leaf and lands with a thud,
Creating a splash in the neighboring mud!

In the thicket, the tales unwind,
Of creatures quirky, gentle, and blind.
Among the whispers, laughter stirs,
Beneath the brush, where magic purrs.

Serenity Wrapped in Green

In a forest deep, where shadows giggle,
Moss-covered stones make the ground wiggle.
Tiny frogs croak their croaky cheer,
While squirrels gossip, their tales unclear.

A snail slides by, with secrets to share,
Waving to flowers with delicate flair.
Butterflies dance, lost in their jig,
Life's one big party, oh so big!

Explorations in the Understory

Adventurers roam, but not very far,
Under the leaves, they spot a jar.
Filled with acorns and perhaps a shoe,
'Whose lost item is this? Do you have a clue?'

Raccoons hold meetings, all wearing hats,
Planning a heist, or just sharing chats?
The tiny world bustles, hilarious and wild,
An undergrowth circus, nature's own child.

Murmurs of Nature's Archive

In whispers of grass, secrets collide,
The great oak chuckles, with branches spread wide.
'What's old man river up to today?'
And the stream just bubbles, 'I'm splashing away!'

Mice take notes as the ants march in line,
'Have you heard the latest? It's comedy, divine!'
With each rustle and swish, the tales come alive,
Nature's own TV, keeping laughs to survive.

Secrets in the Dampness

Under their blankets, the ferns whisper light,
'Is it rainy season or party night?'
The mushrooms giggle, their hats like balloons,
Throwing a bash, with much to attune.

Caterpillars dance in a spiraled parade,
While the damp, squishy ground makes a joyful serenade.

With every squish, and with every cheer,
Who knew hidden worlds lived so near!

Reveries in the Mossy Grove

In a grove where green dreams grow,
Fungi wear hats, oh, what a show!
Bouncy toads hold grand debates,
Arguing over the best pond dates.

A squirrel in stripes, quite the fashion!
Critiques the trees with such passion.
Laughter echoes, a ribbiting cheer,
Mice dance in twirls, sipping root beer.

Stillness as a Canvas

Stillness paints with a brush of glee,
A snail racing down to a flea.
Crickets compose a symphonic snore,
While beetles play cards—just to explore.

A parade of ants in swirly lines,
Tripping over roots and vines.
Each little stumble, a funny feat,
As they search for crumbs—oh, what a treat!

A Dance of Ruins and Renewal

Amidst old logs, the party's hot,
Worms doing the cha-cha—like it or not!
With every twist of twisted fate,
Nature's dance hall—oh, how great!

Moss blankets thrown in wild delight,
Greet the sun and dance all night.
A hedgehog spins, with a wink and a twirl,
"Join the fun!" it shouts, in a fuzzy whirl.

The Heart of the Hidden Grove

In silent nooks where giggles bloom,
Lizards gossip, dispelling gloom.
A leaf twirls down, as if from dreams,
Whispering secrets in gentle streams.

Tadpoles giggle in younger springs,
Croaking frogs with esoteric flings.
Every shadow, with whimsy so rife,
Paints laughter bright in this funny life.

Beneath the Canopy

Under the leaves, squirrels conspire,
Plotting the perfect nut heist, a real fire.
Mushrooms giggle, in twirling fray,
As frogs recite poems by the bay.

The sun peeks through with a cheeky grin,
Tickling the ferns, inviting a spin.
The rabbits dance, in shoes too tight,
While crickets serenade, 'til the night!'

In the Embrace of Shadows

A shadow cavorts, looking for fun,
While fireflies play in an evening run.
The owls hoot jokes with flappy glee,
As shadows gossip, oh so free!

Mice tease the cat, a daring stunt,
With cheese on a platter, they boldly hunt.
In the calm of dusk, laughter soars,
Life's a party beneath the floors.

Tales of Emerald Enchantment

A dancing pixie trips on a leaf,
Laughing out loud, bringing comic relief.
The vines entwine, forming a wig,
As spiders weave webs, way too big!

Mossy beds are a comfy throne,
Where Ladybugs gossip, never alone.
A snail slides by, giving a wink,
As everyone stops for a drink and a stink.

Quietude Among the Ferns

Ferns whisper secrets, soft and light,
While beetles engage in a dance of delight.
Chasing their tails in a leafy race,
Even the mushrooms want a place!

Laughter echoes in the cool, still air,
Echoing chirps, and the lightest flair.
Each leaf a witness to the fun that blooms,
In this green world where laughter resumes.

Reflections in a Dewdrop

In a dewdrop, I see a speck,
A tiny world, what the heck!
Ants parade with tiny hats,
Chasing shadows, and some bats.

A snail's dance is pure delight,
Wobbling left, then taking flight.
Grass blades whisper, secrets found,
Laughter echoes all around.

Ladybugs play hopscotch game,
While petals blush, oh what a shame!
The sun winks, a cheeky tease,
Nature's jest, it aims to please.

In the end, the drop will fade,
But joy's with us, never strayed.
I wipe my brow, feeling spry,
What a ride! Oh my, oh my!

Underneath the Lush Veil

Peeking through the leafy green,
A squirrel's dance is quite the scene.
Acorns bounce like little balls,
While hidden giggles fill the halls.

A hedgehog wears a spiky crown,
Rolling round in nature's gown.
Fungi laugh with funny faces,
In their own unique places.

The brook sings a gurgling tune,
With frogs that croak, their grand monsoon.
Beneath the veil that nature weaves,
Lies a world that never leaves.

When the sun sets, the fun must stop,
But I find joy in every drop.
Underneath this vibrant scene,
Life's a joke, oh what a dream!

Echoes of the Ancient Forest

In the shadow of ancient trees,
Critters gossip on the breeze.
Mushrooms wink with silly pride,
    In their topsy-turvy ride.

The owls hoot out a snarky jest,
While woodpeckers drum for the best.
Raccoons climb with expert flair,
Wearing masks, they stop and stare.

A fairy sneezes, oh so loud,
Sprinkling magic, feeling proud.
The pines whisper secrets, so sweet,
    Laughter trills on every beat.

As night falls, the jokes take flight,
Under stars that gleam so bright.
In this forest, wild and free,
    Joy's the only decree!

Musings of a Soft Bed

In a soft bed of cushy fluff,
Dreams take flight; oh, isn't it tough?
Pillows giggle, curving just right,
While blankets engage in a tickle fight.

The foot of the bed is a jungle green,
Where lost socks gather, a quirky scene.
They whisper tales of every day,
And dance around in a charming ballet.

Even the mattress hums a tune,
Lulling softly under the moon.
A comical snooze, a snort, a yawn,
As night slips by, heralding dawn.

So here I lay, in laughter's embrace,
A world of dreams, a silly space.
With each giggle and slumber's delight,
Soft beds turn chaos into light!

Gentle Caress of the Wilderness

A squirrel in a tux, what a sight!
He's planning a party, oh what a night!
With acorns served on a silver plate,
He's got the woodland dancing till eight.

A rabbit DJ spins with flair,
While the fox cheers him, unaware.
The hedgehogs roll to a funky beat,
In nature's disco, they can't be beat.

Mushrooms glow like disco balls,
As nature's critters have a ball.
The breeze carries laughter all around,
In the wild, such joy can be found.

As dawn breaks in a sleepy grin,
The wild party ends, cheers fade within.
Squirrel tips his hat with a cheeky glance,
In the woods, even the thorns love to dance.

Tides of Time in a Leafy Cradle

A leaf fell down with a sudden puff,
It whispered stories; oh, it's tough!
To carry secrets from years gone by,
As it twirled gently from the sky.

A turtleneck turtle took his time,
While claiming each leaf as his prime.
He'd lean back slow in a sunlit spot,
And ponder if he's missed a lot.

The sparrows chirp with tales absurd,
Like how the wind once lost its word.
With every flutter, tales unfold,
Of mischief woven in leaves of gold.

As dusk arrives, the leaves all sway,
Sharing dreams of a light-hearted day.
In a cradle of green, laughter's sound,
A perfect playground where joy is found.

Beneath the Veil of Verdancy

The grass wears dew like a sparkly gown,
While bugs parade, a tiny crown.
They boast of races, oh what a thrill,
'Til one trips over a dandelion frill.

A wily raccoon, up to his tricks,
Steals berry pies, what a mix!
He giggles and dances, a jolly thief,
While bushes rustle, hiding the grief.

A frog leaps high with a hearty croak,
Chasing butterflies, oh what a joke!
But misjudges the jump and slips with a splash,
Turning the pond into a funny bash.

Underneath leaves where shadows play,
Life's absurdities brighten the day.
In this realm where the silly thrive,
Nature chuckles, oh how it's alive!

Sketches of the Shaded Realm

A snail drew lines on a shady twig,
Creating his art, all real and big.
But every stroke took ages to make,
As a passing ant just laughed and shake.

The trees played hide and seek all day,
Rooted in laughter and games they play.
Sunbeams peeked in to join the fun,
While a squirrel declared, "I've finally won!"

A hedgehog, dignified and stout,
Wobbled and rolled without a doubt.
He's also a prince, or so he says,
With his royal roots in the grassy bays.

In the shaded realm where smiles bloom,
Every critter crafts their joyful tune.
With sketches of laughter, life is grand,
Nature's canvases, a colorful band.

Ode to the Overlooked

In shadows deep where secrets lie,
A humble green that catches eye.
Underfoot, with giggles spry,
It whispers tales as passersby.

With tiny hats made from the dew,
It hosts a tea, all mossy crew.
A party on the sidewalk blue,
While squirrels dance, and birds say woo!

Each step we take, neglect we prove,
They laugh and sway, no need to move.
The ground beneath, a mossy groove,
In nature's jest, they sweetly soothe.

So next time you stroll, take a glance,
At those who wait for a chance to prance.
For every blade, a secret dance,
In the green realm, there's quite a romance.

In the Sway of Tender Green

In the woods where giggles grow,
Soft cushions dance, row after row.
They sway along in breezy flow,
Oh, how they tickle, to and fro!

Upon a log, they shout hooray,
As beetles join the grand ballet.
With wiggly worms, in bright array,
They form a band and sing all day!

When raindrops fall, it's quite the feast,
A splashy bud, a tiny beast.
With every droplet, laughter's lease,
It's nature's joy, never ceased.

So here's to greens that hug the ground,
In belly laughs, they can be found.
With each soft thread, a joy unbound,
In mossy hugs, we're all spellbound.

A Continuum of Quiet Life

In corners dim, where whispers float,
A kingdom small, on life's slow boat.
Where slugs and snails find plans to gloat,
And ponder deep, while crickets quote.

A toad may croak, a tale of yore,
While nibbling ants do jobs galore.
Each mossy patch, a sigil sore,
In laughter's shade, they seldom bore.

With every squish beneath our feet,
They joke that life is oh so sweet.
In colors bright, designs repeat,
Explore their world, so full of heat!

Through every version, time and space,
These little ones still find their place.
With humor sewn, in nature's grace,
A gentle jest, their cozy base.

Mossy Chronicles of the Wild

In tangled woods, the stories bloom,
Of tiny worlds, where critters zoom.
With leafy hats, they hide from gloom,
And craft a life in every room.

A chipmunk's chatter, in the shade,
Shares grand adventures, unafraid.
While moss, the quiet, jokes are made,
In bright green coats, well-displayed.

Through shaded paths, the carpet spreads,
Where giggles bind in leafy threads.
A banquet set for gnomes and reds,
In tales all spun, where laughter weds.

So smile for friends of nature's kin,
For every twist, there's joy within.
In mossy fables, let love win,
A phrase, a pun, where laughs begin.

Luminescence in the Dark

In the shadows, whispers play,
Fungi giggle the night away.
Glowworms dance on pillow mounds,
Nature's jesters, wild and unbound.

Moonlight drips like honey sweet,
With beetles tapping their little feet.
Stars trying hard to steal the show,
But mossy laughter steals the glow.

The Art of Damp Stillness

A snail's race is slow but grand,
Painting paths across the land.
With every inch and slimy trail,
A testament to who won't fail.

Moss sits quietly, plotting schemes,
While frogs leap high, disrupting dreams.
Laughter echoes from the stream,
In this damp world, we all can gleam.

Green Reflections in Twilight

Algae mirrors in twilight's grasp,
Where frogs and fairies dance and clasp.
A whimsical waltz on still pond glass,
With dragonflies zooming, oh what a gas!

Night falls sweet like a soft-spun joke,
As whispers tickle the ancient oak.
The breeze snickers, a sprightly tease,
In hues of green, we bend our knees.

Beneath the Gnarled Roots

Under roots where secrets creep,
The critters gather, they hardly sleep.
A raccoon juggles acorns with flair,
While chipmunks giggle, not a single care.

Mischievous whispers, a woodland play,
"Who's stealing my snack?" the squirrel today.
In this wild riddle, joy does sprout,
Beneath the gnarled, we laugh it out.

Treading Softly on Velvet Earth

I tiptoe on this cushy ground,
Where squished green sponges make no sound.
Each step I take, a silly bind,
My shoe is sucked, my thoughts unwind.

Squishy bits adhere to feet,
Like nature's gum, it's quite a treat.
I laugh while trying to break free,
From this green trap that's clinging to me.

A froggy leaps, it takes a thrill,
In splashes that could flood a mill.
We dance around their silly croak,
As I become a sovereign yolk.

With every springy, squishy fold,
My feet, they dance, they glide, they scold.
On velvet earth, I lose my grace,
And slip into this muddy space.

Memories of the Damp Realm

In memory's grip, where dampness dwells,
I recall the scents of earth's sweet spells.
Fungi pop up like tiny caps,
A version of nature's funny mishaps.

The critters dance with a floppy grace,
In puddles they whirl, in a slippery race.
A worm slides by with a cheeky grin,
Winking at me, oh what a sin!

Drizzle drips down, a soggy cheer,
Each splash ignites a giggle, my dear.
Laughter ripples through murky streams,
Echoing softly my childhood dreams.

As I stroll through this slippery zone,
I'm reminded of how I've grown.
In a world where the damp paths tease,
I find my joy in the muddied breeze.

Gentle Patterns of Nature

In gentle patterns on the floor,
I spot the shapes that nature bore.
The moss, it weaves a green ballet,
A carpet soft where fairies play.

Each leaf, a stick, a froggy face,
Make silly art in a damp embrace.
I chuckle at the vivid sight,
Nature's canvas, pure delight.

A snail meanders with no rush,
Leaves a trail with a daring hush.
I watch in awe, then start to grin,
At how the slugs have joined the spin.

Patterns whisper, softly they call,
In every drop, there's laughter's thrall.
I weave my steps, inspired anew,
In this funny world of greenish hue.

Echoes of Moisture and Time

In echoes soft, where droplets play,
Moisture whispers, come what may.
I hear the giggles of the stream,
Each ripple bursts my joyful dream.

With each squelch, I waltz along,
In puddles deep, I sing my song.
Time seems to pause in this wet domain,
Where laughter falls like scattered rain.

The frogs hold concerts, loud and proud,
Their croaky voices thrash the crowd.
I join in with a silly croak,
In nature's rhythm, I've awoken.

With memories sticky and sweet,
This moist playground is quite the treat.
Echoes dance in the damp delight,
As laughter guides me through the night.

Growth in Forgotten Places

In cracks and crevices, they play,
Whispering secrets, come what may.
Sprouting joy in gloomy nooks,
Telling tales that no one books.

With googly eyes, they seem to stare,
At each passerby, unaware.
Dancing lightly on the breeze,
Tickling toes of roaming bees.

They laugh at concrete, make it blush,
In the city's quiet, joyful hush.
Strutting small, in vibrant green,
A tiny rebellion, so serene.

Underneath the tires' black tracks,
Life springs forth from what it lacks.
Nature's jesters in the grime,
Making beauty out of time.

Shaded Tales of Resilience

Beneath the trees, a party's set,
With plucky ferns, you can bet.
They tell of raindrops, wish on dew,
In a leafy hangout, just for two.

Mushrooms giggle in their caps,
Sharing stories, perhaps some naps.
Winking at the world above,
In a shady dance they dream of love.

Lichens laugh at time's cruel race,
With ancient wisdom on their face.
They sprout and shrug, "We're doing fine!"
In sunlit mornings, they shine and shine.

Here in the shadows, life entwined,
Tales of triumph, never maligned.
A green brigade, in nature's tone,
Celebrating life, fully grown.

An Ephemeral Symphony

On gentle winds, the spores take flight,
A whimsical waltz, pure delight.
They pirouette from tree to floor,
In a flurry of giggles, seeking more.

The honeydew drops make a splash,
As critters scurry, in a dash.
Every leaf's a maestro, so grand,
Conducting nature's merry band.

A chorus of chirps, a laughter spree,
The grass sings soft, a symphony.
Oh, what joy in each tiny note,
As life's orchestra plays from a mote.

But watch your feet, or soon you'll find,
A hidden dance that's well-designed.
Life here's a joke, a playful game,
In this chipper patch, they stake their claim.

Chronicles of the Forest's Breath

In the woodland glade, tales unfurl,
With squirrels gossiping, like a whirl.
Mossy pillows invite a nap,
Such whimsical dreams in a leafy wrap.

The owls hoot out wisecracks at night,
While fireflies join in, oh what a sight!
Each rustle and whisper, a comic play,
Nature's stage, where weirdness stays.

Amid the roots, where shadows creep,
Laughter erupts, in secrets deep.
Twirling mushrooms join the jest,
Adding humor to nature's quest.

So grab a seat on a knobby log,
Join in the fun with a happy fog.
In every corner, life's a jest,
A green-tinted laugh fest, at its best!

The Unseen Harmony of Nature

Among the leaves, the critters chat,
Squirrels in bowties, imagine that!
With acorns as hats, they plan a ball,
In the grand tree trunk, they dance and sprawl.

The ants hold meetings, all very formal,
While a lazy worm dreams, it's quite normal.
Frogs croak their wisdom, quite loud and wise,
As fireflies twinkle like twinkling eyes.

A snail in a hurry, on a skateboard zooms,
While the daisies gossip, sharing their blooms.
Each blade of grass in a quirky pose,
Nature's own sitcom, anything goes!

And when the moon peeks, with a cheeky grin,
The nighttime shenanigans truly begin.
With giggles and whispers, the forest sings,
Unseen harmony, oh, nature brings!

Voices of Verdant Shadows

In the depths of green, laughter and cheer,
Where the tigers wear stripes, and not a fear.
A parrot tells jokes, in a high-pitched tone,
While a chameleon laughs, in shades of its own.

The mushrooms, they giggle, sprouting up tall,
As raccoons throw parties, and invite them all.
With popcorn of seeds and a soda of dew,
In the shadowy woods, fun never feels blue.

Beetles parade in their shiniest suits,
While the grasshoppers dance in their finest boots.
A wise old owl calls out, "Who's ready to play?"
In the voices of shadows, they brighten the day.

And as the sun sets, throwing colors around,
Fireflies ignite, in a shimmering sound.
The forest forms chorus, in a jubilant tune,
Voices of green, in the light of the moon.

The Fabric of Time in Green

In the patchwork of leaves, the clocks twirl and spin,
As squirrels debate, who gets the first win.
With needles of pine, they stitch up the day,
Creating a tapestry, bright in display.

The trees tell stories, of ages gone by,
With rings full of laughter beneath the blue sky.
The breeze carries whispers of things that once were,
As fern fronds wiggle and gently concur.

Bees hum a tune, while spinning their thread,
In the loom of the flowers, where lazy bugs tread.
With petals like fabric, they fashion their dream,
In this world of green, where time flows like cream.

Every moment is woven, with giggles and cheer,
In the fabric of nature, the joy's crystal clear.
While dandelions wink, in their playful delight,
The sun smiles in, bidding goodnight.

Ceaseless Cycles of Renewal

In the cycle of life, the sun plays its part,
While daisies spin tales, of many a heart.
The seasons, they giggle, rotating around,
As leaves drift in laughter, twirling to the ground.

Winter brings snowflakes that giggle and dance,
While squirrels in cable knit jump at the chance,
To build up a stash, and hide it away,
Planning a feast for a warm sunny day.

Spring bursts with laughter, as blooms take a peek,
While frogs jump in puddles, splashing in streaks.
And as summer laughs loud, with sunbeams aplomb,
The garden throws parties, what a fresh calm!

With autumn's embrace, the harvest arrives,
All creatures unite, in their colorful lives.
Ceaseless in cycles, this fun never ends,
In the tapestry woven, where nature transcends!

Thickets of Timelessness.

In thickets thick where time stands still,
The squirrels plot with utmost skill.
They hoard their acorns with a wink,
While mushrooms giggle, making us think.

A tortoise told a tale so grand,
Of how he became a rock band.
With crickets drumming and frogs on keys,
They serenade the buzzing bees.

The wise old owl takes up the stage,
With a nightcap on, he's quite the sage.
His jokes are cheesy, and that's no lie,
They leave the other critters high and dry.

In this lush realm, so wild and free,
Even the trees have jokes, you see.
So join the fun, don't be a bore,
In thickets everlasting, there's always more!

Whispers in the Gloom

In shadows deep where whispers creep,
The mushrooms dance, while willows weep.
They share their tales in hushed delight,
Of nighttime mischief and silly fright.

A raccoon reads a map upside down,
While owls hoot from the tallest crown.
Echoes of giggles fill the night,
As fireflies flash in pure delight.

In the gloom, a hedgehog spins,
Making bets on who can win.
"I'm faster!" says the crafty hare,
But all know he's paws-itively rare.

With each hushed tone and secret laugh,
The forest holds its quirky craft.
So join the whispers, night-time throng,
In tales of laughter, you can't go wrong!

Secrets of the Forest Floor

The secrets lie beneath the leaves,
Where beetles giggle and the spider weaves.
A dance of dust, a waltz of worms,
In their tiny world, the laughter churns.

A tiny ant with dreams so big,
Plans a party with a funky jig.
With twinkling eyes and a feather hat,
Each critter comes, imagine that!

The toadstool stage is set just right,
As fireflies twinkle in the night.
The forest floor is a comedy show,
With laughter rising, ebb and flow.

So tread with care, don't squash the fun,
Join in the revelry, everyone!
For in this chaos, joy is found,
In secrets whispering all around!

Lush Chronicles in Green

In lushest groves where stories bloom,
The plants gossip, dispelling gloom.
A vine tells tales of adventurous days,
Of tree-top races in sunlight's rays.

With creatures dressed in vibrant hues,
They hold a party, it's hard to refuse.
The chattering birds lead the parade,
While butterflies dance, unafraid.

A cheeky raccoon plays peek-a-boo,
With a startled frog that hops right through.
The laughter echoes, fills the air,
In this green haven, without a care.

So wander deep where laughter's rife,
In chronicles lush, and full of life.
With nature's joy and whimsical team,
Together we'll weave the wildest dream!

Celebration of Quiet Corners

In a nook where whispers dwell,
Sneaky spiders weave their spell.
Pinecone parties raise a cheer,
In the quiet, joy draws near.

Dirt is dancing, mossy glee,
Squirrels break out rand' dance spree.
Acorns tumble, oh what fun,
In their world, we're all but one.

Shhh… the crickets start to croon,
Whilst the toads play a soft tune.
Laughter echoes through the leaves,
Such a riot, no one believes!

And in corners, laughter hides,
In these tiny worlds, it glides.
Join the feast of silence nu,
It's a bash, just me and you!

In the Stillness of Growth

Mosses giggle, stretching wide,
While toadstools form a platform slide.
Each sprout is a jolly prank,
Coloring the world with their rank.

Sneaky roots make their own rules,
Whispering secrets to the fools.
Nature's party, oh so bright,
In the shadows, pure delight.

Daisies join, a lively crew,
Boozy bees must sip their dew.
With each bloom, a riot begins,
In the calm, where laughter spins.

Watch the leaves play hide and seek,
With giggles that seem quite unique.
In the stillness, fun unfolds,
As the green tale truly molds.

The Color of Silence

In quiet glades where shadows dance,
Colors bloom in happenstance.
A tinge of green, a splash of cheer,
In silence, laughter's always near.

Rolly-polly bugs abound,
Mossy carpets wrap the ground.
Nature laughs, it's quite the scene,
Painting the world in shades of green.

A snail slides by with great finesse,
Half a shell, no need to stress.
While others rush, he takes his time,
In slow-motion, it's sublime.

Sitting still beneath a tree,
Join the giggles quietly.
In colors vibrant and quite fair,
Silence sings, life's a rare care.

Being Among the Green Tapestry

In the tapestry of greens,
Life unfolds in silly scenes.
Frogs on lily pads take a leap,
While flowers giggle, secrets keep.

Leafy whispers float in air,
Silly shadows everywhere.
Toads wear crowns, they rule the fest,
In nature's realm, they jest the best.

Little critters share a laugh,
Chasing tails on a leafy path.
In this green, the world's alive,
Where nature's humor truly thrives.

So come along, don't be shy,
In silence, watch the moments fly.
Among this quilt of earth and sun,
Every corner's full of fun!

Nature's Silent Testaments

In a damp corner, secrets lie,
Mossy whispers, oh so sly.
Tales of frogs that leap with flair,
And slugs who slide without a care.

Underneath the shaded boughs,
Nature's quirks make us say 'Wow!'
A snail races - well, it tries,
While ants debate the meaning of pies.

With every step, a squish or two,
What's that smell? Well, who knew?
Mossy carpets, laughter's call,
Nature's giggles, big and small.

So pause and ponder, take a look,
At every cranny, nook, and crook.
Join the fun, let worries cease,
Nature's jokes bring sweet release.

The Green Tapestry of Memory

In a world of green, they gather 'round,
Mossy patches, secrets abound.
Forgotten dreams from days of old,
Mystic tales that must be told.

A frog in a hat croaks quite loud,
While mushrooms dance, a playful crowd.
Squirrels in suits, what a sight,
Trading acorns 'til the night.

The carpet of green shares its glee,
Painting the ground like a jubilee.
If you listen close, you'll hear a song,
From nature's stage where all belong.

So chuckle softly, join the cheer,
For mossy mischief is ever near.
The stories linger, bright as a spark,
In the green tapestry, life leaves its mark.

Surrender to the Earth's Embrace

Beneath the trees, the moss does glow,
Inviting weary feet to slow.
If you sit and take a breather,
You may just find a dancing weaver.

A worm in a tie takes center stage,
While beetles argue about their age.
Mossy mats are soft as pie,
Even shy critters can't deny.

With every tickle from the ground,
The whispers of nature will astound.
A snail's salute, a mushroom grin,
Join the fun, let laughter begin.

So lay back, let nature tease,
In the embrace of the earth, find ease.
Life's simple joys, both big and small,
Are wrapped in green, inviting all.

Chronicles of the Earthbound

Underfoot, the chronicles spread,
A riot of green where dreams are fed.
Mossy tales in every fold,
Of sunny days and raindrops bold.

The ants have formed a union strong,
While crickets sing the evening's song.
A snail writes notes to a busy bee,
In a love letter made from leafy debris.

With each small step on the earth's soft floor,
New stories arise, a joyful uproar.
Fungi gather for a comedy show,
While shadowy figures dance to and fro.

So tiptoe lightly, hear the cheer,
In this green realm, no need for fear.
Chronicles bloom where laughter's found,
In the light of joy, we're earthbound.

The Language of Lichen

In a forest chat, they say,
Lichen love to lounge and play.
They whisper jokes on bark so thin,
While mossy mates join in the din.

They argue over who is best,
The green or gray, it's quite a quest.
With fungi laughing as they roam,
They call the trees their cozy home.

Each color tells a funny tale,
Of rainy days and sunlit gales.
As they sip dew in morning light,
Their banter makes the world feel bright.

So if you see them on a walk,
Join their laughter, hear them talk.
For plant life holds a humor grand,
In their tiny, leafy wonderland.

Stories Woven in Greenery

Amidst the leaves, a tale unfolds,
Of clumsy critters, brave and bold.
A snail ran fast with all its might,
Yet tripped on roots and lost the fight.

The acorns giggle in a pile,
As squirrels leap with quirky style.
Each nut a dream to plant and grow,
They toss them high, just for show.

The ferns all whisper ancient lore,
While bouncing beetles ask for more.
With every rustle, a new plot spins,
In nature's book where laughter wins.

So when you venture through the green,
Listen closely, see what's seen.
The stories hide beneath your feet,
In every nook, there's joy to meet.

Life's Quiet Resilience

In cracks of concrete, greens have sprouted,
The tiny plants speak loud, no doubt about it.
They wiggle through the stone and grime,
Singing softly in rhythm and rhyme.

When storms hit hard and winds do howl,
A mossy blanket wears a scowl.
It laughs at weather, takes its stand,
A patch of peace in a tumultuous land.

The petals dance, though oft they bend,
With quirks of nature, they'll not pretend.
Each blossom holds a secret smile,
In trials faced, they still have style.

So when you feel like all is lost,
Remember greens that pay no cost.
They thrive in silence, strong and true,
With funny quirks just waiting for you.

Nature's Hidden Manuscript

Beneath the shade, a script lies bare,
With stories told in fresh cool air.
The grass writes notes in swaying style,
While flowers chuckle all the while.

In tangled vines, the gossip grows,
Of critters who misplace their clothes.
A caterpillar once got caught,
In a web of yarn that spiders bought.

Bamboo laughs as it sways along,
Its hollow heart a playful song.
With whispers soft upon the breeze,
It shares the giggles of the trees.

So venture close, and take a peek,
At nature's tales, both fun and cheek.
For in the wild, the laughter rings,
In every line, the joy it brings.

The Allure of the Forgotten

In the attic lay a shoe,
A relic of a dance or two.
Mice parade in finest tails,
Judging all the dusty trails.

Old books don't read themselves, you see,
While jumping spiders sip their tea.
A sock, a thought, a rogue old hat,
Each lost to time, where did they scatter?

The spoon that once stirred broth and stew,
Now scoops up dust—a ghostly hue.
A clever cat with knowing eyes,
Laughs at all these sweet goodbyes.

Chasing memories round the room,
With quirky joy, they chase the gloom.
In this land of what was right,
Forgotten things now spark delight.

Echoes of the Earth's Memory

Whispers float on zephyr's breath,
From ancient trees, a quiet depth.
A worm in tweed, so brave, so bold,
Shares secrets that never get old.

The stones once walked, in tales they tell,
Of dancing rains and frogs that fell.
Each pebble giggles, each twig winks,
As nature plots her little zinks.

A puddle's splash, a sudden quack,
Reflects the sky, the clouds' hijack.
The chatter of ants in a frantic line,
Singing praises for sweets divine.

With quirky beaks and silly ways,
The critters plan their finer days.
Echoing laughter, both loud and keen,
In the forest, where all is green.

Under the Benevolent Shade

Beneath the great old willow tree,
Squirrels gather round for tea.
Acorns stacked in a wobbly pile,
Weaving tales with a cheeky smile.

The moss spreads thick, a velvet mat,
Where butterflies take turns to chat.
Bored bees hum a lazy tune,
As dandelions dance to the moon.

Laughter bubbles from the ground,
Magic whispers all around.
With shadows playing peek-a-boo,
Nature's stage—where fun ensues.

In this grove, where dreams collide,
We nap and snack with elf-like pride.
Under the shade, we doodle and scheme,
Creating a most whimsical dream.

Nature's Secret Librarian

A tree stands tall, a page unturned,
With whispers of the world, it yearned.
Its bark tells tales of sun and rain,
Of little critters and their gain.

The roots are scribbled lines that weave,
Stories only the now can leave.
Rabbits hopping, owls that hoot,
Memories gathered—nature's loot.

In the quiet, secrets bloom,
Among the ferns that softly loom.
Each leaf a page, each breeze a sigh,
Informing all who wander by.

With laughter ringing through the air,
The forest holds its treasures rare.
A librarian, though often shy,
Shares stories whens the stars are nigh.

Whispers Beneath the Canopy

In the woods where the squirrels play,
A mushroom waved, 'Have a nice day!'
A flower giggled, petals aglow,
'This breeze tickles, don't you know?'

Beneath the leaves, a snail held court,
Telling tales of a leafy sport.
'Last week I raced a leaf in flight,
I won, but it took most of the night!'

The whispers danced, as shadows pranced,
With critters all in a merry trance.
A frog declared with a mighty ribbit,
'In my kingdom, I'm quite the spirit!'

So if you wander with spirits' cheer,
Catch the giggles, lend an ear.
For nature's folly, warm and bright,
Sprinkles laughter in daylight's light.

Linger of Green Shadows

In a patch of grass, a bug did waltz,
'The wind's quite brisk, so don't blame me, faults!'
He spun and twirled, his legs all a-buzz,
'Let's dance on dew, just because!'

A twig stretched out, and tossed a wink,
'This party's great! Come join, don't think!'
While leaves overhead had their own debate,
'Is it bad to hang out till it's late?'

A chipmunk chimed in, cheeks stuffed with snacks,
'We can party hard; who needs to relax?'
The shadows laughed, in darker hues,
As insects played their rhythmic blues.

With every rustle, more friends would come,
Beneath the stars, the forest hummed.
A night of giggles, and silly feats,
In the realm of green, joy never retreats.

Secrets in the Damp Earth

In earth so rich, a worm did muse,
'What's life like above? Give me the news!'
A toad replied with a croaky jest,
'It's mostly bugs and the occasional pest!'

The ground shook as a beetle strayed,
'Life's a thrill ride; don't be dismayed!'
Shouted the ants, their line in a rush,
'With teamwork here, there's never a hush!'

A thistle boasted, 'I'm pretty tough!'
'You may be prickly, but not so rough!'
The laughter bubbled, a low, gentle sound,
While secrets whispered all underground.

In damp corners, a party ensued,
With friends from the soil, the mood was renewed.
So if you dig deep, don't take it for granted,
You'll find a world where the vibes are enchanted!

Chronicles of the Verdant

Adventures unfold in a leafy tome,
Where the dandelions wish to roam.
A clever breeze flipped the pages bright,
'You've got to see this! What a sight!'

With twigs as swords, the brambles staged wars,
While the daffodils cheered from front row floors.
'Triggers and tactics, bring on the fun!'
She cheered as her petals basked in the sun.

Unruly vines swayed, reliving their tales,
Of daring escapades and gusty gales.
'We swung from the branches, with glee we soared!
A wild ride, though our leaves are now floored!'

So scroll through these pages, laugh and delight,
In the chronicles spun by the green of the night.
For nature's a storyteller, gallant and grand,
With tales of the leaves, and its infinite band.

Hidden Lives Beneath the Canopy

Underneath the leafy vines,
A raccoon wears sunglasses and dines.
He flips through a book, oh what a sight,
Laughing with squirrels 'til late at night.

An owl shared gossip with a wise old tree,
Who juggled with acorns, oh so carefree.
Squirrels rapped rhymes, took turns to boast,
While fungi held a mushroom toast.

The worms have fashion, in soil they strut,
Spinning their tales, oh what a cut!
Ladybugs dance, on petals they glide,
While ants play poker, full of pride.

So much drama hidden from view,
In the forest's heart, life's not so blue.
Nature's a sitcom with each twist and turn,
Underneath the canopy, oh, how we learn!

Nature's Silken Tapestry

In the garden, the spiders weave,
A tapestry bright, oh you wouldn't believe.
The beetles parade, all shiny and bold,
While ladybugs gossip about tales untold.

The flowers are giggling, swaying with glee,
As butterflies chat over raspberry tea.
With petals like pages, they share their dreams,
A secret world bursting at the seams.

With sounds of the forest, so comical too,
A raccoon joins in, with a kazoo.
The shy little toads, with dance moves so slick,
Try to impress with their hopping trick.

In this woven world, laughter does bloom,
Where every tiny creature lights up the room.
Nature's a quilt, stitched tight with delight,
A funny tableau beneath the twilight.

The Weight of Forgotten Memory

Old roots whisper secrets from days of yore,
Of critters and laughter, behind every door.
A snail claims to know where the treasure is hid,
While frogs croak about the friends that they bid.

Porcupines reminisce about parties they missed,
With excuses so wild, they can't be dismissed.
The fireflies blink, holding tales of the past,
While fungi dream of a fun feast they cast.

The bark has a tale of a long-lost shoe,
Tripping young foxes that thought they knew.
Geese in formation, honking their tune,
Reflect on memories beneath the moon.

The weight of the past hangs light as a fluff,
For nature's a jester, it's never too tough.
In laughter we learn, and through tickles we grow,
As forgotten memories continue to flow.

In the Footsteps of Time

Dodging the shadows, the ants march ahead,
With breadcrumbs of wisdom, they make their bed.
Each twig has a story, lined up in a queue,
While the crickets compose, a nightly debut.

The trees lean in closely, sharing their views,
With whispers of seasons and all their hues.
A "who stole my acorn?" echoes the hall,
As life scrolls along, in great comedic sprawl.

The river gurgles, as if it's in jest,
Flowing with laughter, never a rest.
Stones hug the shoreline, making a fuss,
While time ticks away in a frantic rush.

In this wacky world, where moments align,
Giggles and chuckles intertwine with time.
So tread lightly, friend, on this jolly path,
For in every step hides nature's warm laugh.

The Subtle Touch of Growth

In a garden where quirks take flight,
A plant tried pants—what a sight!
Chasing shadows, it danced with glee,
Swaying to tunes of a bumblebee.

A rumor spread, the leaves turned green,
With fashion tips from the garden queen.
They wore hats made of dew and grass,
Confidently strutting, they had class!

Who knew that roots had such a flair?
In soil they'd mingle, gossip to share.
With every sprout they'd crack a joke,
While bright sunbeams laughed till they spoke.

So next time you glance at the flora,
Remember the giggles and the aura.
Every bud can bring some cheer,
In the quirky kingdom of greenery here.

Paths Less Traveled by Sunlight

In the forest, a snail took a trip,
While whispering secrets, it gave a quip.
With a backpack made out of bark,
He journeyed onward past the dark.

"Why rush?" he said to the passing bee,
"Take a breath, come wander with me!"
Together they laughed at squirrel's sprint,
As they watched the shadows begin to tint.

But oh, the bumblebee felt the sting,
Of a dandelion who claimed the spring.
"Just wait," said the snail, "I've got a plan,"
As the flower folded, "I'm more than I am!"

With petals that danced in the cool soft air,
The friends trod lightly without a care.
Each giggle a thread in the sun's warm weave,
In paths uncharted, they learned to believe.

Beneath the Veil of Growth

There's a tale hidden 'neath the soil,
Where carrots giggle, and peas like to spoil.
Their leafy stories twist in the breeze,
Whispering laughter through the tall trees.

"Did you hear the one about tomato's plight?
He slipped on a turnip, what a funny sight!"
The lettuce chuckled as dawn broke through,
With misty giggles, in morning's hue.

Kale told jokes with a twirl of its leaf,
While chives played tricks, oh what a thief!
Beneath the veil of mist and of dew,
The veggies grouped up for their morning brew.

"We'll sprout a show this summer," they cried,
With laughter and sunshine as their guide.
In fertile laughter, they grew with pride,
A garden of jokes where joy would reside.

When Stillness Speaks

In the quiet of dawn, the mushrooms conspire,
To share little tales of raucous desire.
They tickle the roots with their whispering charms,
While nearby the hedgehog snoozes in arms.

"Do you believe how the daisies engage?
They hold their meetings—what a strange stage!"
Their gossip echoed in the misty light,
As slumbering wonders began to take flight.

And with every giggle, the garden did bloom,
While busy bees danced, avoiding the gloom.
A turtle remarked, "It's a slow life we lead,
But still, I find joy in the simplest of seed."

From the stillness arose a raucous sound,
As creatures awoke from their slumbering mound.
In nature's own rhythm, they'd find their own beat,
Where laughter can sprout, and stillness retreat.

Beneath the Weight of Dew

Beneath the weight of morning dew,
A snail slipped by, a race to pursue.
With every slip, he giggled loud,
While grass blades mocked from a leafy crowd.

A ladybug joined with her red cape,
Swaying side to side, she tried to escape.
"It's just a drizzle!" she called with glee,
As a drop of water splashed her with spree.

The earthworms danced in a muddy ball,
Whispering secrets, they felt so tall.
In the morning light, they wriggled around,
Claiming their turf, without a sound.

And while the sun peeked over the hill,
The antics of critters were quite a thrill.
Laughter erupted, as nature conspired,
In this world so lush, they never tired.

The Tranquil Embrace of Moss

In a cozy nook, the moss did snooze,
With tiny critters sharing their views.
A toad softly croaked, his voice like a hug,
While ants played tag on a stout little bug.

A chipmunk stumbled, thought he was sly,
But slipped on the green, oh me, oh my!
He tumbled down in a fit of giggles,
And mossy cushions broke his wiggles.

A butterfly flitted, graceful and proud,
Whispered to friends, "I'm the best in the crowd!"
But then got stuck in a thick mossy weave,
And laughed through her struggle, "Oh, I won't leave!"

With every joke and a turn of fate,
The world was a circus, no time to wait.
In this embrace where the liveliness grows,
Moss cradled laughter, as only it knows.

Harmony in the Untouched

In the untouched corners of the grand old wood,
Squirrels held meetings, they were so good.
Chattering loudly, they planned their escapades,
While ferns rolled their eyes at their noisy parades.

A wise old owl hooted, "Keep quiet, my dears!"
But the ravings and rumbles faded his cheers.
A vixen suggested, "Let's dance and prance!"
And the whole forest burst into a chance.

Mushrooms popped up, in colors so bright,
Joined the soirée, a marvelous sight!
But each time they tried to break into song,
A bear with a snore would claim it was wrong.

So the creatures decided on a whispery tune,
And under the stars, they swayed with the moon.
Harmony bloomed in nature's delight,
With laughter and friendship, here every night.

The Soft Carpet of Nature

Upon the ground, a soft carpet lay,
Bouncing with joy as critters would play.
A hedgehog rolled in, all covered in leaves,
Spinning around, he tickled the eaves.

A raccoon rummaged for snacks, oh so sly,
But slipped on a moss mound and let out a cry!
"Next time, I'll tread with a bit more care,
Or dance on the edges, if I dare!"

Fireflies twinkled, a disco ball glow,
Inviting the critters to join in the show.
They twirled and jumped, with rhythm and cheer,
While the wind whisked them around, "Come on, don't fear!"

Nature's soft carpet, a stage for delight,
Where the day turns to mischief and ends with bright night.
With laughter and whimsy, each moment gleamed,
In this playful enclave where everyone dreamed.

Voices of the Forgotten Grove

In a grove where the trees wear bright, leafy hats,
The squirrels hold conferences on springtime spats.
A rabbit debates with the bugs on the floor,
While a wise old owl snickers, 'Oh please, not more!'

The mushrooms all gossip in colorful tones,
Trading tall tales of their spore-laden zones.
With laughter that echoes, they brighten the day,
In the dance of the leaves, they just love to play!

Remnants of Rain and Time

Puddles hold secrets and dreams of the sky,
Where frogs croak their odes, and the raindrops comply.
A snail named Larry believes he's the king,
Though the puddles retreat, he still wears that bling.

Clouds whisper stories of places they've seen,
Of dancing with lightning, so bold and so keen.
With every soft drizzle, new jokes come alive,
Together they giggle, ensuring we thrive!

The Quiet Growth of Resilience

In the shade of a bough where the shadows sit tight,
A tiny green sprout hugs its soil, feeling right.
It dreams of the sun but fears the loud rain,
Yet dances with droplets, embracing the grain.

A wise worm named Fred gives advice that is neat,
'Embrace every trial; it's all quite a treat!'
With roots dug in deep, they all come alive,
Finding joy in each struggle, together they strive!

Tangles of Nature's Memory

In a tangle of vines, where the breeze likes to tease,
The critters recall when they danced with the trees.
A squirrel lost his hat to a gust of delight,
While the birds laugh and chirp at his funny plight.

The ivy cracks jokes with the old twisted oaks,
As they reminisce over their old, silly hoaks.
They weave through the past with a giggle and twist,
In the tapestry of nature, nothing's amiss!

Tread Lightly on Emerald Dreams

In the forest where whispers creep,
Tiny critters dance, the secret keep.
With each step we giggle and sway,
Watch out for the mushrooms on display!

A squirrel in knickers, what a sight,
Chasing shadows in the fading light.
Beneath green canopies, we tease,
Nature's jesters, bringing us to our knees.

A frog in a bow tie, oh so grand,
Conducts the crickets with a wave of his hand.
While fireflies twinkle like stars in flight,
We laugh, we frolic, till the fall of night.

So tread lightly on dreams that gleam,
In emerald patches of a joyful theme.
With each giggle, let worries unwind,
Nature's comedy awaits us in kind!

Poetry in the Patches of Life

Amid the moss, a carpet soft,
Pickles and penguins, oh, what a scoff!
We scribble verses in vibrant green,
Life's little quirks, what a scene!

A ladybug with a dash of flair,
Wearing tiny glasses, beyond compare.
Tickling toes as the daisies sway,
Moments like these, they make our day.

From acorns dropping with a thud,
To ants in line, marching in mud.
Each stanza unfolds with laughter and cheer,
In nature's gala, we find our sphere.

So gather 'round, let silliness bloom,
In patches of life, there's always room.
For joy and whimsy in every turn,
In the mess of the wild, we have much to learn!

The Embrace of the Underbrush

Beneath the leaves, we creep and crawl,
Stumbling on treasures, giggles call.
With twigs as swords, we wage a fight,
In a kingdom of green, filled with delight.

A hedgehog flips, oh what a spin,
Curled up in a ball, can't let you in.
With mossy hats and sticks for swords,
Noble knights of nature, demanding rewards.

Bushes whisper secrets, oh so sly,
About a turtle wearing a bow tie.
As we play hide and seek with the rest,
In underbrush secrets, we are blessed.

So dance through the thickets, skip and sway,
In vibrant embrace, let joy have its say.
Together we roam, the silly and spry,
Under the green, where laughter can fly!

Tales from the Ground's Embrace

In the ground's embrace, there's fun galore,
Worms tell tales, who could ask for more?
A gopher in a hat, quite the sight,
Playing peekaboo from morning till night.

The ants have thrown a grand parade,
Marching with pride in a leafy glade.
With a grand finale, they wave their flags,
While a butterfly laughs, in colorful rags.

Mushrooms rustle, they gossip and chat,
While bees dance around, how about that?
In every corner, a story hides,
Of laughter and life where mischief abides.

So gather round, hear the laughter swell,
In the tales from below, where spirits dwell.
With nature's confetti, let joy replace,
Every dull moment in the ground's embrace!

www.ingramcontent.com/pod-product-compliance
Lightning Source LLC
Chambersburg PA
CBHW070320120526
44590CB00017B/2751